YELLOW

Reem Al Mubarak

AUSTIN MACAULEY PUBLISHERS™
LONDON · CAMBRIDGE · NEW YORK · SHARJAH

YELLOW

Reem Al Mubarak

Copyright © Reem Al Mubarak 2022

The right of **Reem Al Mubarak** to be identified as author of this work has been asserted by the author in accordance with Federal Law No. (7) of UAE, Year 2002, Concerning Copyrights and Neighboring Rights.

All rights reserved. No part of this publication may be reproduced, stored in a retrieval system, or transmitted in any form or by any means, electronic, mechanical, photocopying, recording, or otherwise, without the prior permission of the publishers.

Any person who commits any unauthorized act in relation to this publication may be liable to legal prosecution and civil claims for damages.

The age group that matches the content of the books has been classified according to the age classification system issued by the National Media Council.

ISBN - 9789948825630 - (Paperback)
ISBN - 9789948825623 - (E-book)

Application Number: MC-10-01-9185483
Age Classification: E

Printer Name: iPrint Global Ltd
Printer Address: Witchford, England

First Published 2022
AUSTIN MACAULEY PUBLISHERS FZE
Sharjah Publishing City
P.O Box [519201]
Sharjah, UAE
www.austinmacauley.ae
+971 655 95 202

Table of Contents

The bitter truth...55

Let it go..79

I am lost...117

Shooting stars...154

The givers...170

It will pass..177

A letter to my father..191

A letter to the ones we miss...194

This book is dedicated to my family who always believed in me.

This is dedicated to my friends who pushed me to the edge of accomplishment.

This is dedicated to you, dear reader, to mend your soul and warm your heart.

YELLOW

A dream of mine shined brighter than flames,
A dream to change thoughts into words,
A dream where letters were changed into poetry,
Here I am in once a dream and now in your palms.

Never be ashamed of having a soft heart. Not everyone has the courage of feeling the energy of those around them; not everyone has a heart that is gentle as yours.

You are courageous in your own way.

YELLOW

You've planted a seed in me and watered
it ever since. You've slowly made it
grow until its roots were spread down my soul,
making me full of you.

YELLOW

I am sorry for promising you that I would never leave,
I intended on keeping that promise, I really did. It was
until it started haunting me down, wrapping its strings around
my neck, suffocating me and forcing me to stay,
even when I was unhappy. I was a jar full of wonders, little did
I know you were sucking all that I had in me. I promise you
something I know I can keep; I promise you I'll be a room full of
love once you're gone.

Find me there.

Find me where true artistry is born,

Where the blues and reds intertwine, and where the purples and oranges spill.

Heartless

How could I be heartful when my heart was taken away?

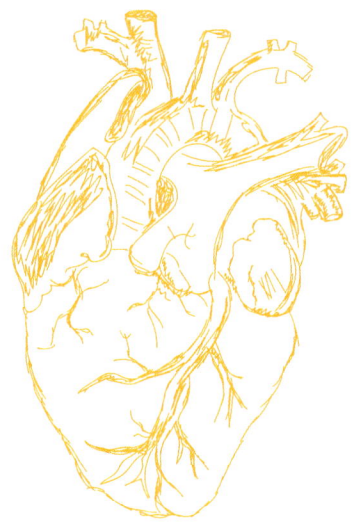

YELLOW

She was an angel formed as human, sent here to make our lives better. Her wings were taken, concealed in a place she didn't know of. She couldn't fly, but she was able to teach them how. She was pained but made them heal.

I am strong as a mountain, and you knew that. You just chose to frame me in your eyes as if I was a fragile whole that could fall into pieces at any moment.

You have loved me regardless.

The number of times I've been told not to care as much, and not to be too nice to people because it'll ache eventually, is countless. But here's the thing, I might be too caring, and not being hurt is an uncertainty, people are unpredictable, and they have every right to be. But I am willing to take the risk and live up to the chance. If being too nice could make a soul feel worthy, if I can help an empty soul feel something, then I am willing to get hurt. I am willing to get hurt because at the end of the day when I redo it all over again, my heart will mend.

YELLOW

Bring happiness, honesty, respect, and kindness to someone's table for one day the table may turn, bringing you back all what you once offered.

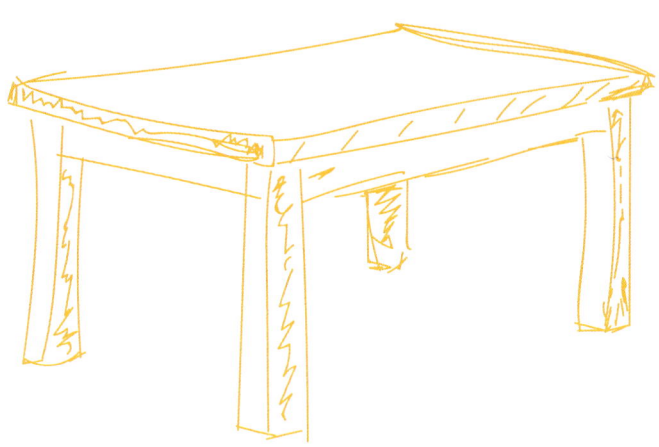

YELLOW

Do not tie me up to you just because you uncovered the deepest parts of me. Just because you unlocked the most secretive doors in me does not mean you own me. I allowed you to do so, it was me who let you, it does not give you the right to stand in my way, it does not give you the right to keep my key with you. It does not mean you get to stand on my light and cast it with your shadow. I don't belong to you, I belong to me, so get out of my way and let my soul go.

YELLOW

You are the key to my happy place.

You are broken you said with that pity voice of yours
I was not broken nor torn
I was a cracked girl with hopes in her tears
You are too much to handle you said
I was not too much nor too confusing
You were simply too less for me.

YELLOW

Your flaws painted you beautifully.
Every edge of you made me wonder, will
I ever find a canvas as beautiful as you?

A soft soul with a puppet heart wrapped around your fingers.

To figure out a puzzle, to follow two steps is what you should do. Never look deeply into a piece, that is when you'll stare at the flaws of the paperboard. Never look too shallow for your eyes may see nothing but the pieces that are out of place. Look into your life the way you fix a puzzle, not too close yet not too far, only then the beauty of your own life shall conquer your eyes.

She is kind enough to please everyone around her but neglects herself.

You are the mountains that keep my world safe from hurricanes and volcanos.
You are the ocean that carries my secrets deep under. You are the stars that lead me to my missing pathway.

YELLOW

You are so mesmeric.

I kept you hidden from everyone else knowing that the world will never understand the masterpiece you are.

YELLOW

Listen to the love hidden in-between the voices of your parent as you argue.
Open your eyes to all what they gave up on to raise you.
Appreciate all what they have built to care for you.

You are who you are because of them.

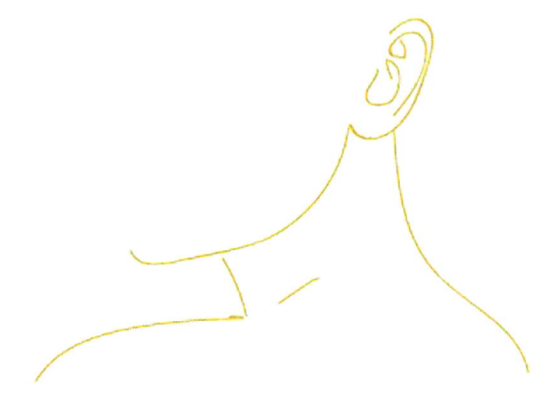

YELLOW

Learn to forgive those who mistreated you
You say you do
You may smile to them too
But deep down you've grown an ache
I know forgiveness may seem a sign of flaw
But I promise you it is sign of perfection too
The strength forgiveness beholds shall help you grow
I think it's time for you to let go.

Go on and on for hours about who you are, share the stories behind the scars your soul carries. I promise you I will listen to every word you have to say. I will hold on to them and love them. I will not wait for you to love me back; I love you enough and have more love inside that is waiting for me to set free.

She was never conscious that she was changing the world more than what she had intended.

You are not good enough keeps ringing in my ear like a bell. I cannot seem to put the little voice in my head to sleep nor find a way to shut it out once and for all. It is stopping me from moving forward, I never knew words could chain my feet down this way.

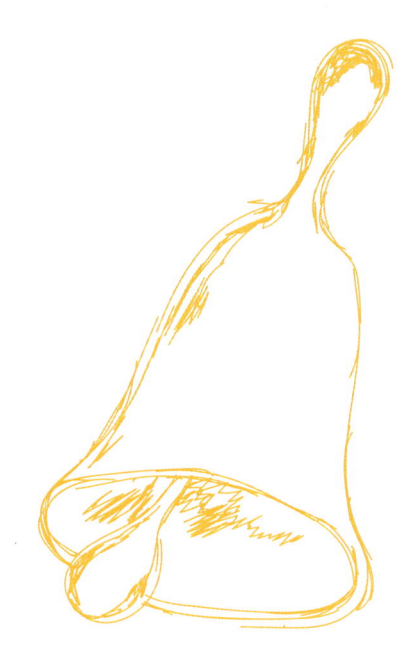

Beautiful had been misused, it somehow lost its worth between all the meaningless things people often tell each other. But you, oh, you have made this word beam with its true colors, you made every letter it beheld make sense.

You are truly beautiful, my dear. I could rest my eyes on you eternally.

Empires are being burned down
inside me, arrows aiming to my
heart. Little did they know a storm was hitting, turning
my soul into a quiet battlefield

We were mixed together like paint, creating artistry we weren't aware of.

YELLOW

You are unlike any other. What made you special is the sweetness that runs through your veins, it is the kindness that beats with your racing heart, it is the thoughts that could surmount everything in seconds. What fascinates me once more is that you are never aware of what you have in you.

YELLOW

The flag:

Ever felt your heart dropping then coming right up? Pounding like never before?

Feeling the rush of fear swimming in your flesh?

Feeling the coldness as it numbs your toes?

You are fearfully falling for a heart that is begging.

YELLOW

You do not fit in a world like this and you never will. It is not because you are not good enough, it is because you are far too good. You are beautifully out of place like a waterlily in the middle of a desert.

The Bitter Truth

The bitter truth about losing someone is that it never gets better, it only continues to ache as you miss them more each and every day. You teach yourself how to live without someone you've counted on your entire life. You might wake up thinking they're still around because of how real a dream felt, but reality pulls the rug from underneath your feet. When you try to remember how they looked like, or try to remember the echo of their voice, how they left comes rushing back, and it shatters you all over again. It's like a constant burn in your soul, you try so hard to put down or hide until you realize putting it down is not an option, so you try getting used to it. You try to get used to the fact that you were once complete but have to continue living incomplete. You live in constant fear of being abandoned, so you make sure everyone else feels secure, and you try to fulfill the souls of everyone around because you never wish such feeling upon anyone. You work so hard to make everyone feel complete because you know how much it hurts being without. But it's okay because you know you have loved them unconditionally when they were around, and the realization of that puts you at ease, and you continue to love them forever.

YELLOW

I will make sure your world knows no darkness nor grays,
I will paint your rainy skies pink and angry oceans yellow,
I will fill your empty voids with joy you never felt before.

A sunflower was once found,
Found stranded in a desert full of sands,
A desert where she thought she didn't belong,
She wished for sands into green heavens to turn,
She closed her eyes for a night full of restful sleep, with a moonlight peck on her cheeks,
She slept with hopes in her heart, and dreams of painting dried out lands with colors never seen.
To bumblebees' rhythms she rose,
She opened her eyes to see empty lands, into green heavens they transformed,
Heavens painted with love like never before,
She looked closer, and a lost petal-less lily was found.
She whispered into her ears, and the petals grew anew,
She smiled to her new heaven and realized she was finally where she truly belonged.

YELLOW

With every situation you unlock more doors inside you, you discover more of who you really are.

Of all the mysteries
You are the only one I wish to solve.

YELLOW

You've grown to be a building in my chest
With rooms that can set me on fire,
Others can sweep wonders down my lungs.

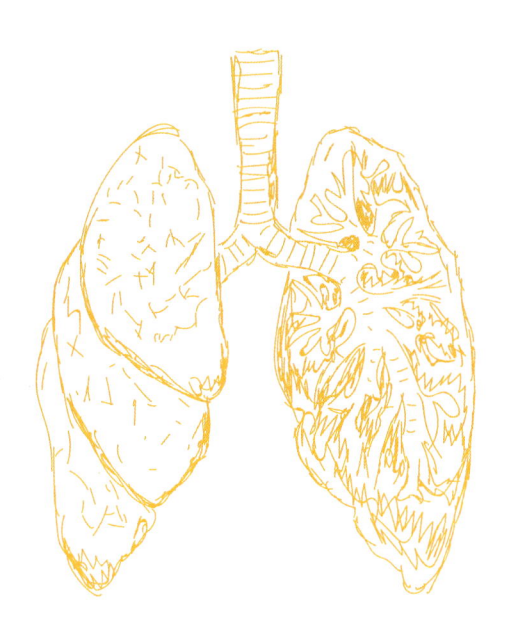

YELLOW

Whenever I close my eyes, I see words and letters wandering around my soul. I can feel passion my heart is seeking.

They told me time heals everything,
So I looked up to the hanging clock and said,
"Heal me,
Heal the hole that is inside me,
Heal my broken heart,
Oh, dear clock, please heal me."
The clock ticked, telling me that nothing could ever replace the feeling that I was loved entirely. The clock ticked again, telling me to lift my chin up for the day shall pass and another form of love would take place, reminding me that there is enough love out there to fill my holed heart.

YELLOW

Let me look at you,
Let me travel in your veins and pursue what interests you,
Let me paint your hair with my fingers the way sun does,
Let me record the echo of your laughter with my ears,
Let me stop time and talk to you for hours until time is in our hands,

Let me love you like you've never been loved before.

True love is when your backbone belongs to someone. I am madly in love with a womb that carried me patiently, with arms that held me so close to her chest, I could hear the pounding of her kind heart. I am in love with that soft blow over my knee after I had it wounded, I am in love with arguments that hid love like no other.

You are my heart, Mother.

My mind created mysteries no one could solve; talking about them only made me realize how much they ache. I knew I had to lick my wounds on my own. It was my battle to fight no one else's. I felt things I have never felt before, they were simply too heavy for my shoulders to carry. I held a brush mixing vibrant colors, hoping some might spell over my dullness. I was praying for my soul to return, and that is when my fingers started linking letters, creating words that turned into poetry; that is when my soul took a step closer. Poetry was born, and a lost soul returned, reminding me that within my worst self, I came back to life.

YELLOW

How is it that I have legs but cannot seem to walk?
How is it that I know how to swim but only seem to drown?
How is it that I have a heart but cannot seem to feel?
How is it that I have a voice but cannot seem to talk?

Your past memories are reminders that mistakes you have done along the way are motivations to help you with your upcoming journey, they are reminders to keep your door open and behold, for beauty might be on its way.

YELLOW

Your happiness is in your hand.
Believe in something extraordinary,
Laugh until your tummy aches,
Allow your heart to feel every edge, even sharp ones,
Let your feelings be,
Love yourself, but mostly, love life.

I look at you and my heart screams,
You look at me and my heart quiets,
I smile to you and my heart races,
You smile to me and my heart drops.

You drowned me with confusion until I taught myself how to swim,
You dragged me through insanity, but darling who said I was ever sane?

YELLOW

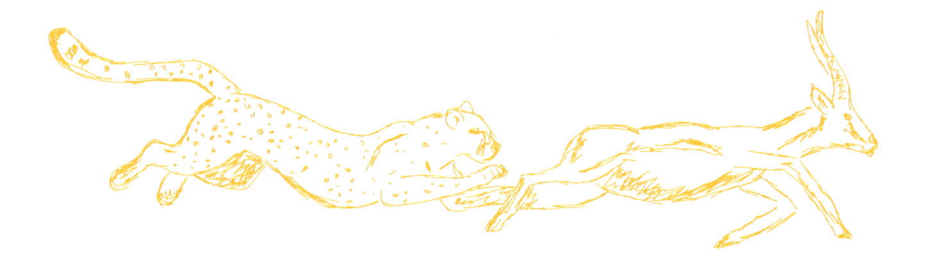

Chase your dreams the way a predator chases its prey, run after them the way a cheetah races after a gazelle.

Reach your dreams and own them, they are yours.

Waiting for a flower to bloom all winter, that is what a blessing feels like. It is making every struggle beautiful as a petal during spring.

Let It Go

If you keep going back to the people that were intentionally removed from your life, you will be stuck in a time loop you have created. There is no reason for you to look back and confuse yourself, there is no fun in going back to bad habits, they are not worthy of you, let it go. What is meant to be yours will wrap itself around your fingers on its own.

One of the most liberating decisions in life is dedicating your time and energy on trying to be the best version of yourself and deciding to pull away from small talks, gossips, and people who don't add up anything to your soul or the world. Start loving the world we live in and try your best to give back rather than paying attention to the pollution certain people create. Life isn't perfect, as a matter of fact, nothing is, and we should never expect it to be if we're not even halfway there. There will be sharp edges that we'll be forced to walk over sometimes, but that's okay because sharp edges are not all that's there in the world. There is a portion of people in life who might hurt us or try to spill terrible things along the way, and that's okay too. Because horrible people are not all that exists in this life, we just have to look elsewhere and manifest our time into becoming better humans, doing so will slowly make the change we've all been looking for.

YELLOW

I know letting you go would mean a piece of me is going too,
I know I would continue to wish for you upon many shooting stars,
I know it'll hurt despite pretending it never mattered,
I know we were never meant to be,
But I decided to grasp on to that one percent of hope that things might take a turn.

YELLOW

Love is like water, put it in a container and watch it form. You were put in my heart and formed yourself exquisitely.

YELLOW

I would create roads and pathways for us to meet again.

YELLOW

The shy stares from afar sent signals that have lost their way,
The little glances spoke of so many stories waiting to be loved,
The deep gazes revealed treasures that were hidden for so long.

YELLOW

YELLOW

I wonder how life would be with no hope,
It would be like a sky with no hanging stars.

Nothing can heal a gapped heart, a gap that was created after the loss of someone,
Nothing can replace the feeling of knowing you were loved unconditionally, and now it is all gone.

Here I am hugging the memory of you, praying to meet again.

YELLOW

I know that you are no longer here, inside me knows
that this is for the best. I know that when you were around, I
loved you enough and I don't want you back because I
regret things or wish I have done things differently. What
I am grieving about is the fact that I have grown so much
love for you and have no idea where to pour it. I cannot
seem to find a place for it, since it grew just for you. Your love is
roaming inside me, slamming doors, waiting for you
to respond with no use, knowing that you are no longer
here to respond anymore. I cannot explain the banging of doors
that is happening inside me, I cannot describe the numbness I
am feeling.

I cannot say it out loud admitting it will only make it hurt.

I stared at the mischievous blue whispering quietly, "You are too mesmerizing to be mischievous." It wrapped its waves around my waist dragging me under replying, "Only those who fear me find me mischievous, so tell me, do you?" Bubbles echoed out of my mouth as I said, "Never, Blue."

And when walls closed in,
backs turned, and hands let go,
When hearts ached, and tears no longer shed,
When home was lost, and grounds were lifted,
I found myself between your arms.

You are a fairytale that knows no beginning and no end, I am a character that is seeking between the lines of your beautiful story, falling in love with every word, every typo, every chapter and every picture.

YELLOW

I am longing onto the memory of you, replaying the vague echoes of your voice as it sinks gently down my soul. Trying to find the right words to describe you is the hardest thing as nothing seems to do you justice, and no one else's words would ever fit you.

YELLOW

You were an abandoned building that made my soul curious, I took a step into your first room, and that is when it hit me that I'll be haunted forever.

I was enchanted by you.

Till forever finds its end.

YELLOW

I was your moon but you had your eyes set for the stars.

Tell me why of all people it is me you chose?
Mumble to me all what made you fall for me,
Make me love me the way you do.

YELLOW

You showed me more of you each day,
That made me love you more and more,
Until there was no turning back.

When the night was silent and people were asleep,
Her head felt empty but heart, oh, so heavy.
She scooped it out to have a talk,
"Poor thing why are you aching," she asked.
"You extend me too much,
You hand me over to those who constantly break me when I'm already cracked,
I know you mean well but sometimes the world doesn't," it replied.
She gave it a peck while gently placing it back when it was sound asleep.
So her mind woke up, and she stayed up all night.

Even though you were the reason I had to pull my heart out at certain times, I cannot deny that you are the reason it beats the rest of the time.

It shattered me like a missile
through a glass window.

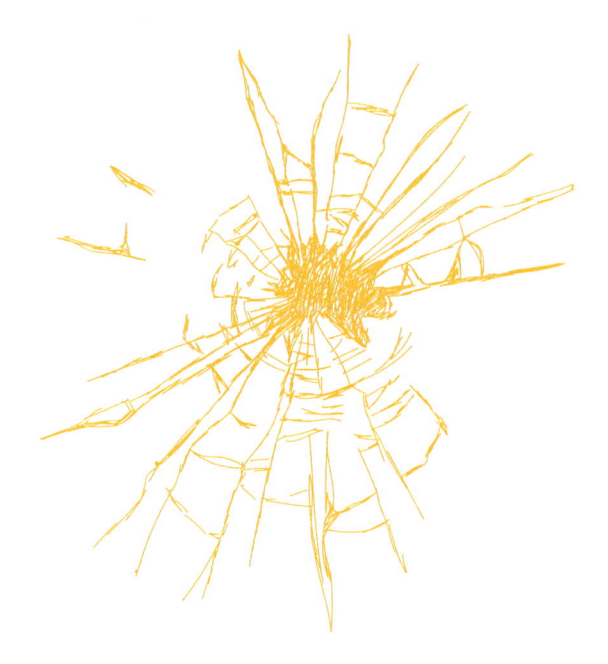

They gathered around the table,
Talking and sharing thoughts.
She, the talkative one, found herself quiet,
They looked at her while she was smiling to the moon, Thinking she was absurd, they asked:
"Why are you looking at the moon this way?
Why are you glowing?"
She looked at them, then back at the moon,
Smiled as she softly answered:
"Because the moon is the only permanent thing in a world that is continuously spinning,
It's the only thing that never gets bored of my nonsense,
It's the only thing that listens when the rest had their ears wide open but hearts shut,
It's the only thing that exists to make life better when we humans can't promise to do the same."

YELLOW

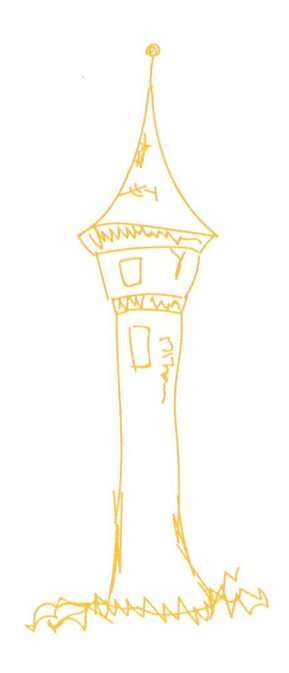

Was it the exquisiteness of your face that
made me a prisoner in your tower?
Or was it the magic of your soul?

What a beautiful incident it was when my eyes met yours,
What a beautiful incident it was when the only voice I remembered was yours,
Oh, what a beautiful incident it was when the only heart I wanted was yours.

YELLOW

I Am Lost

Walking around, searching for a way out of this maze,
Searching for the heart I dropped by mistake,
Searching for the mind I have misplaced.

YELLOW

Will I ever see you in my dreams?
Will we ever meet again?
Will you ever fill me with the words I ought to say?
Will I ever tell you how much I have loved you?

YELLOW

At the end of daylight, as the sun was wallowing its yellow rays into the white clouds saying goodbye for the day,
I found myself wishing for you.

YELLOW

A soul between the sky and grounds,
A heart between poetry and art.

YELLOW

I've chased a million sunsets, but none of them is close to what runs through your eyes, heart and soul.

My heart spoke louder than all the words out there,
It spoke of the memories we've shared,
It spoke of the love that is roaming inside me, not finding a place to settle in anymore,
It spoke of you, and how you slipped right through my fingers before I could ever fix my grip.

It is not just the excitement that you make me feel,
It is something else,
It is the peace you bring along,
It is how you make every single bit of me sit still, and
you're the only one that has ever made me feel this way.

I felt that lash falling on my cheek,
I pressed it hard with my finger hoping the harder I pressed,
the quicker my wishes to be true,
I closed my eyes and wished,
I wished for the clouds to be touchable,
I wished for the stars to fall into my lap,
I wished for the moon to grab my hand and lift me up high and hold me tight,
I wished for time to freeze and be mine,
I wished for every sorrow to wither away,
I wished for your love, I wished and wished with all the air my lungs carry.

YELLOW

And that's why I call her a shooting star,
She's once in a lifetime kind of person,
I closed my eyes to wish upon the few fleeting seconds
she dances across the sky,
Little did I know her ears were wide open with a smile kissing my wishes true,
And she turned into a forever-hanging star in my sky.

A peculiar leaf was swept from its grounds,
It was swept by the cold winds of winter lands,
Swept for miles away from its ground,
It was carried, swirling in between the clouds,
It was until the winds grew apart that the leaf fell,
Gently swaying in between lands and skies, dancing along the rhythms they create,
It fell till it reached the grounds of unknown lands,
It looked around in the middle of unfamiliar paths,
It looked and there it was, another peculiar leaf was found,
And that's when they both realized what a beautiful journey it was and yet to be.

YELLOW

I loved you enough when you were around
I love you enough that you are gone now,
I even loved the grief that came along,
I love you yesterday, today, tomorrow and always.

A year full of high and low tides, going back and forth thinking it was easy to let you go, thinking I could simply scoop you out of my heart like ice cream. It was until I realized you are my memories, you are my home, I cannot take a step forward without bringing you along.

We are inseparable, and I know that now.

YELLOW

"Butterflies are envious of your beauty,"
you whispered in my ears

Standing in front of a mirror wondering,
Will I ever recognize myself again?
Falling into a hole whirling and feeling nauseous,
Will I ever find my way back?
Voices in my head whispering my failures over
and over again, *Will I succeed still?*
I looked around and saw that beautiful child
with a leer that was contagious,
I kneeled down as she rested her tiny fingers
alongside my cheeks,
I closed my eyes to capture the moment,
When I had them reopened, it was all gone,
the doubts, nausea, and the whispers.
It was all gone, with just a little bit of hope.

You are always there, I may not see you, but I know
you're still there, looking after me while standing in the corner,
making sure the road has no cracks for me to
walk over. You are always there clapping softly over my success,
quietly waiting for me to shine.

A star that never wanted to shine without you.

YELLOW

How is it possible to speak of the beauty galaxies behold when it is you I am looking at?

Respect your boundaries,
Sometimes the answer ought to be no so say it,
Stop outspreading yourself, if you do, you will have nothing left of you to offer.

I kept wrapping folds around my eyes, choosing not to believe, closing my eyes from what was hurtfully true. You have let go of who you are and I cannot recognize you anymore. You hurt my heart more than anyone could, and it is me to blame. I shouldn't have exposed the depth of my soul to you. I chose to ignore my heart when I knew perfectly that of all my senses, my heart was the strongest.

YELLOW

We were like fuel and match,
We completed each other by igniting flames,
We were both irreparable, one would burn, and the other would be burned,
We knew being together was toxic, yet fell in love.

Appreciate the effort someone makes; you never know what they went through just to make you happy.

YELLOW

Many people in the course of a lifetime have peeked into me,
None have put my chaos at ease, but you,
You make my heart beat softer than it ever could.

I walked over the warm sand as I felt my feet sink under,
I felt the misty breeze the waves tossed on my face,
I looked at the ocean and asked, "Will you take me along?"
"Didn't they tell you mischievous is what I am?" he replied.
"You're far too dazzling to be mischievous, Dear Blue."
Waves wrapped around me like a blanket as they slowly pulled me under,
I opened my eyes and saw life as the sun was kissing the drops of water,
I learned to breathe underwater,
The deep blue is now my home.

They often wonder how I seize the good in everyone.
Let me tell you a little secret, *a devil can too be an angel with just a leap of faith.*

YELLOW

I seek refuge in you the way a baby holds a fuzzy blanket against his cheeks during breezy nights.

YELLOW

"I love you more than anything," you said.
I smiled and murmured:
"No one loves me more than the Sun and Moon,
They follow me no matter how far I go,
Drawing a grin at day and wiping tears at night,
Exposing colors at day, and illuminating darkness at night,
Filling me with hope at day, and putting me to rest at night."

You smiled and said," You are my Sun and Moon."

Shooting Stars

Certain people in life are a little different from everyone else. They try their best to fit in, but they can't seem to find a way no matter how hard they try, and that is not because they are less, no, not at all. It's quite the opposite, you see, they are far more. These people are what I call shooting stars. They come once in a lifetime. You may spend years wishing for one or upon one, and if you're lucky enough, they listen to your whispers and wish for you too. When they do, an immense amount of beauty will unveil itself before your eyes. When you get closer to them, it is as if you've gone to another universe, a place that makes you feel seen, a place where your soul is understood and loved, it is a place that we are all unconsciously longing for.

They are sent here to fix the broken pieces of this world intentionally, but they start small, they begin with people. They fill you up with hope, warmth, love, kindness, but most importantly, they fill you up with belief. They inspire you to become better and spot the potential that is buried inside you. They are the type of people who believe in you with all their hearts. They push you and support you without asking for anything in return. They help you grow wings and teach you how to fly just when you're about to believe you are ordinary. When you meet one of those people, your life changes, these people are too rare that some began believing they don't exist, but they do. So, when you meet your shooting star, hold them tight, wish upon them, and never let them go.

I am in the middle of a fight between a mind and a heart. A fight where the mind is fearfully reminding me to be cautious, not to give what I cannot replace to everyone who hands me a smile. A fight where the heart is forcefully telling me to go back to those who had it ached, pushing me to get my scars reopened.

YELLOW

Stop expecting things from others, stop getting your hopes up for people who gave up on believing in themselves a long time ago, you don't owe them that. You are the main character of your story, you are who's important. You get to steer your life in whichever direction you want, stop waiting for others to steer the wheels for you.

YELLOW

The way your brain work takes me on a journey I never want to return from.

You're an angel,
You're an angel with flames in that red hair of yours,
You're an angel with galaxies in those black eyes of yours,
You're an angel with stars in those freckles of yours,
You're an angel with radiance in that porcelain skin of yours,
You're an angel with sunlight in that smile of yours,
You're an angel with beauty in that sweet soul of yours,
You muttered.

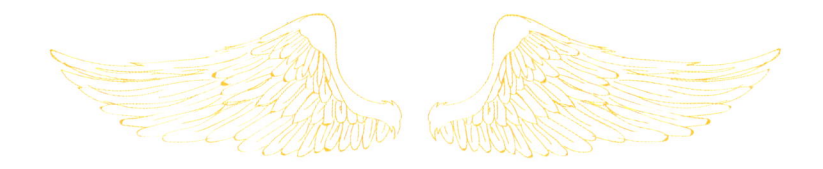

And when I'm missing you, I look up to the sky with a tearful eye and a hopeful heart to meet again.

Some days may be frustrating, just like the autumn season, taking away every leaf a tree held on to. Other days are just gloomy, they freeze your soul the way winter freezes twigs. Then comes the spring, growing back not only leaves but blooming flowers too, feeding the tree with hope. Other days are bright and happy the way summer is, painting the true colors of a tree, showering it with warmth and peace.

You my dear are a tree, not the leaves,
Days pass by the way seasons do,
They affect the leaves, but never the tree.

"Do you love me?" you asked.

"Darling, I never knew what love felt like until my soul met yours."

The Givers

Let me tell you something about some people who are walking this earth right now. These people require little and offer so much, they give out so much of themselves and often too many times. They were told a dozen times not to give what can't be replaced to whoever passes by, not to give their hearts to whoever hands them a smile, and not to give out so much when given too little in return. But, no matter how hard they try to listen, they can't do so, and they continue to give. No matter how much they give out, they still carry so much more inside them waiting to run loose. These people carry gentle hearts that get shaken up by the slightest wind that comes their way as it shatters them entirely, so they shove their sorrows deep down into places that are out of reach, and their lips are sealed shut.

And that's okay because they heal differently, you see, they don't require much talking, and their only source of healing is through people, through you. They selflessly run towards those who are aching to fill them up with warmth until their pain is eased. They run towards those who feel empty to fill them up with love until their souls find their way back. They witness peace in the well-being of others and find joy in the success of their loved ones. They mend with the love that they spill over others, and that is their power. They come into your life only to make sure everything is in place, to make sure your wings are unclipped, and when you're ready to fly, they let you go, and that's when their sorrows are gone.

YELLOW

Let me stare at your eyes as the sun is setting,
Let me look for the softness that swims in you,
Let me gaze at those black eyes of yours
as they slowly turn brown, telling me that even inside that
heavy soul of yours, gentleness lives,

Let me watch your warmth reveal itself.

The kindest love of all is when that pitch of yours slowly change as we argue,
The most genuine love of all is when your eyes sparkle along with my success,
Love at first sight was when the door slammed open and your smile met mine,

Your love is the most treasured thing I have encountered.

There is rhythm in the wind howling,
Melody in the leaves flapping,
It is magnificent hearing them whispering
in your ears, telling you there is more to
the world than what your eyes may see.

It Will Pass

Listen carefully to my whispers and what they are trying to say, beautiful heart of yours will restore, that alluring soul of yours will find something new to grab on to. That grin of yours will soon turn into a chuckle.

My whispers are never untrue.

YELLOW

As the sun was stretching her first rays,
And the waves' melodies arose,
And the clouds were dancing in between,
My heart was swept away in the middle of it all.

Into the forest, she went,
She dove between trunks that leaked stories,
She wandered ready to collect some that might spill over her,
She walked until her legs went weary,
And under an ancient tree, she sat.
She rested her head on the warm trunk of a tree, murmuring:
"Tell me your secrets, oh old tree,
tell me everything about you,
let me cruise your veins, and relive everything you've witnessed."
The tree took a deep breath, you could hear the cracks of her wooden skin as her chest expanded answering:
"Should I tell you of all the secrets I've listened to? All the stories I've lived? Or all the ones I wish to have lived?"
"Tell them all, ancient tree,
Tell me everything lurking between your ribs,
Tell me what that chest of yours is carrying,
Tell me all about the whispers you continue to shush,
Tell them all to me old tree,
my heart is yours to lend," said the girl.

YELLOW

The closer I get to you, the more at home you make me feel.

An enigmatic familiarity that I found in no one else but you.

Feel the joy while blowing bubbles, hear them pop as they splash soap in your eyes, leaving them shut, making you wonder how many colors a person with closed eyes can see. Feel your cheeks ache after that grin you had, hugging your heart with bliss like never before. Gaze at that golden gleam a sun forms as it warmly kisses your lashes. Inhale that astounding smell of grass right after it rains, creating a forest in between your ribs. Memorize a baby's first cry while realizing life came to life.

It is the little things people overlook are what makes life elated.

You were away all the time, I forgot what it felt like having you around.

I cannot tell you out loud for I fear you may not understand,
Look closely into my eyes, listen carefully to what they are trying to say, they are aching to be heard,
It is the second your eyes decide to meet mine,
That is when all that is unspoken of starts revealing.

Wishing to be heard.

YELLOW

They often wonder what makes clouds so special?
What makes her heart full of them?
They are just air and water, they said.
Little did they know, clouds were her hope,
They were the only ones looking down at her when she was looking up with an empty heart,
They slowly found their way into her soul, and that is where they settled ever since, *making her full of them.*

YELLOW

My love for you will always find its way to you,
it will find its way to you when oceans dry out,
and skies are no longer blue.

A Letter to My Father,

It all started when you heard the first cry and realized that within life came your life,

You held my hand as I clasped my tiny fingers around your thumb,

You taught me that there will always be more hidden inside me waiting to be unleashed,

You raised me with patience and a smile that puts my storms at ease,

You wrapped me, protected me and shielded me until I grew up to be someone who made you stand tall with pride,

You showered me with love that I can't recognize anywhere else but within you.

YELLOW

I will always feel safe knowing there is a moon out there making darkness look beautiful.

A Letter to the Ones We Miss

To the dear ones, the ones that made us complete, to the forever loved, the honest and pure ones. The ones that made life brighter with magical skies and eyes filled with bliss. To the ones we've lost unexpectedly or slowly at a time when they were needed, loved, and presence always wanted, here is a letter to you.

Our love for you is embedded within us when we're sitting in the middle of a crowd with voices around and stomachs aching from all the laughs. The love is rooted when our eyes suddenly decide to shed along with the thought of you, or when we try to recollect memories spent with you. Words lost their shape, and our love for you took another form that grows along every little infinity hiding between the bitter and sweet moments we continue to live without you. When we decide to turn the little dreams we once whispered to you into tangible realities, it is because you inspired us to do so and all we wish for is to make you proud. You're always there at the back of our heads, clapping softly over every successful step we take, and the remembrance of the remembrance of that keeps us going.

Thank you, dear ones, for all the memories, thank you for giving us a taste of true love, and thank you for the feeling of safety and completeness you brought along throughout the fleeting years you've spent here. Thank you for being angelic. Thank you for making our days, months, and years heavenlike.

YELLOW

I wish I could flee this world and take you with me,
I wish we could create a world of our own,
I could take you along to an alternate reality,
A dreamlike reality that's ours to keep,
A world where you could be the sun to my skies, and I'll be the clouds to yours.

THE END